Making Crayons

by Judy Kentor Schmauss

 HOUGHTON MIFFLIN HARCOURT

PHOTOGRAPHY CREDITS: (c) ©William Thomas Cain/Stringer/Getty Images; 3 (b) ©William Thomas Cain/Stringer/Getty Images; 4 (b) ©Joel Sartore/National Geographic/Getty Images; 5 (b) ©Zoom Team/Shutterstock; 7 (l) ©William Thomas Cain/Stringer/Getty Images; 8 (b) ©M Neugebauer/Corbis; 10 (r) William Thomas Cain/Getty Images

Printed in Mexico

ISBN: 978-0-544-07230-5

7 8 9 10 0908 20 19 18 17 16

4500607972   A B C D E F G

Contents

Vocabulary	Stretch Vocabulary
property	factory
temperature	molds
texture	containers
melt	harden
	pigment

Introduction

What is your favorite color of crayon? Did you know that there are millions of crayons made every day? That's right, millions. You can go to a crayon factory and see how they are made. Or you can read this book!

Some factories can make more than two million crayons a day!

The Science Behind Making Crayons

Crayons are made using simple science. As you know, anything that takes up space is matter, and matter has different properties. Size and weight are properties. So are temperature and texture.

You can change the properties of a liquid by freezing it or warming it.

Remember that matter changes if you change one or more of the properties of matter. What happens when you freeze water? It turns to ice. What happens when you put ice in the hot summer sun? It melts.

Heating and Cooling the Wax

Candles are made of wax. Crayons are made of wax, too. Crayon wax goes into a large metal tank. What do you think will happen if the wax is heated? When the temperature gets high enough, the wax will turn into a liquid.

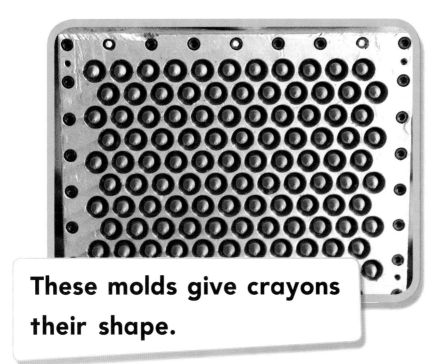

These molds give crayons their shape.

The melted wax gets poured into molds. The molds are containers that are shaped like crayons.

Next, the molds go into cold water. The cold temperature makes the melted wax cool and harden. Open the molds and what do you have? Crayons!

Changing the Color and Shape

A crayon's color goes in next. The color is called pigment and is a powder. The powder is poured into the melted wax and mixed around.

Factories make about 120 colors of crayons.

Which crayon is easier for you to color with? Why?

Your first crayons might have been fatter than the ones you use now. Fatter crayons are easy for small hands to use. Crayons come in many sizes and shapes. That's because crayon molds come in many sizes and shapes. Liquids do not have any certain shape. Liquid wax takes on the shape of its container.

Wrapping the Crayons

The crayons come out of the molds after the wax hardens. Special machines spread glue on paper. Then the crayons are wrapped in it. Machines do the wrapping. Special machines spread glue on the paper. Other machines wrap this paper around the crayons. Still other machines put the crayons in boxes. Crayon boxes come in all sizes.

These crayons are nearly ready to leave the factory.

Using Old Crayons

You can make your own rainbow crayons!

- Peel the wrappers off old, broken crayons. Put the crayon pieces into a mini-muffin tin.
- Ask an adult to heat the oven to 135 °C (275 °F) and put the tin in the oven.
- Ask the adult to take the tin out of the oven after the colors start to run together.
- Cool the tin for 25 minutes. Then refrigerate the tin for 5–10 minutes.
- Turn the tin over onto a dish cloth.

Freeze It

Investigate how the size of a mold affects freezing time. Place water in different-sized containers. Predict which container will take the shortest amount of time to freeze and which will take the longest. Freeze the water. Write about what you learned.

 Step It Up!

Draw a picture that shows the steps involved in making crayons. Write a sentence that explains each picture. Then share your picture with a friend.